50 T[

Traveling to India

Manidipa Bhattacharyya

CZYK Publishing

Lock Haven, PA

Introduction

"If there is one place on the face of earth where all the dreams of living men have found a home from the very earliest days when man began the dream of existence, it is India!"
- Romaine Rolland

India has been considered the land of dreams since a long long time. People are mesmerized by the natural beauty of this land, the simplicity of life of its people, the vibrant colors of culture and creativity. The spicy food and mystic spirituality pulls people from around the world to come here and explore. As most tourists say India is not a country it is an experience. Take your time to find out about the country and discover yourself in the process.

From the mighty Himalayas to the merged waters of the Arabian sea, the Bay of Bengal and the Pacific ocean. From the dry desserts of Rajasthan to the lush green forests of Arunachal Pradesh. There is a treasure trove of places to explore and experience. Every place has its unique cuisine, its own art forms, a different cultural and linguistic identity and its own religious flavor.

In this book we have tried to put together the bare essentials you need to know before travelling to this country. The people who have travelled to India have all left richer. Some have come to love the country so much that they keep returning at every opportunity. Hope to meet you soon on some road in India.

Table of Contents

24. Avoid Street Food

25. Enjoy A *Thali*

26. Enjoy A Home Dinner

India – Customs, Etiquette And Propriety

27. Dress Appropriately

28. Follow Instructions At Tourist Places

29. Remove Shoes At Entrance To Temples

30. Cover Your Head At Religious Places

31. Forget About Personal Space

32. Understand The Interesting Head Wobbles

33. Learn The Local Language

34. Interacting With The Opposite Sex

35. Be Careful With Your Hands And Feet

36. Understand That Time Is Relative

37. Feel Like A Celebrity

38. How Much To Tip

39. Be Part Of The Festivals

India – Safety Norms

40. Display Your Wedding Band

41. Avoid Going Out At Night

42. Raise Your Voice

43. Be Prepared To Fight Back

44. Refrain From Carrying Too Much Cash

45. Keep A Calm Head

46. Keep Your Mobile Handy

India – Shoppers Stop

47. Explore Before Buying

48. Ship Purchases Home

49. Enjoy Bargaining Like Indians

50. Know What To Buy

Dedication

I dedicate this book to my motherland - India.

India Fact Sheet

1. Check Your Visa Requirements

People from most of the countries are required to have a valid visa to enter India. This is a lengthy paper work process and need to be finished before travelling. Recently however, India has expanded visa on arrival for 43 countries including US, for tourist who are visiting for less than 30 days. Crosscheck your travel dates and the visa requirements properly before travel to avoid unnecessary bureaucratic trouble.

To travel to certain parts in India like Arunachal Pradesh, one is required to get special permission. The visa on arrival might not qualify you to get these permits. If you have plans for visiting any place that requires special permission then you should get a regular visa.

2. Know Your Money

The Indian currency is the Indian Rupee. The largest bank note is for ☐.1000 followed by ☐.500, ☐.100, ☐.50, ☐.20 and the smallest is ☐.10. Earlier there were smaller denomination notes for ☐.5, ☐.2 and ☐.1 which are no longer printed but some of the old issues ones are still in circulation. The smaller denominations are available as coins starting from 50 paise, then ☐.1, ☐.2, ☐.5 and also ☐.10.

ATMs are widely found in the cities and towns. However, if you are travelling to remote places like hills and villages check with the locals about the availability of ATMs. Some places have hour long queues at the ATMs!

Credit Cards are accepted at all big hotels and shops. If you are staying at budget hotels find out from the reception if they accept credit cards else pay by cash.

3. Know When To Travel

India experiences extremes of weather changes. Being such a huge country the weather differences across the country varies a lot as well. While northern India gets extreme of heat and cold the southern part experiences intense heat all round the year. The rains or the monsoons hit the western Kerela coast by end of May then continue to move inland to cover the rest of the country for the next few months. During this time many areas in the East, North East and some bigger towns are flooded, landslides are common together leading to a communication standstill. By around September the monsoons start receding from the northern parts of India. Rains continue on the south eastern coast caused by the retreating monsoons. November to March are the dry months with pleasant weather across the country. This time of the year even the southern states experience a relatively less intense heat. The peak trekking season in the Himalayas are however in August September while the rest of the country experiences rain.

4. Know What The Time Is

This very huge country has only one time zone. The time difference is 5.5 hours ahead of GMT/UTC. The concept of day light savings does not apply here.

India - Accommodation And Transportation

5. Plan Your Holiday

India is a very vast country offering a variety of travelling options. Choose wisely what you would like to explore, cramming too much in too little time will only exhaust you. There are mountains, rivers, seas, desert, rainforest and much more. Then there are religious places, spiritual places, fun places, business places. Figure out what kind of holiday you are looking for and then make the choice of places.

6. Plan Your Travel

Once you have the list of places to visit chart out your travel path. Find out about the means of travel and time required to travel. You can do this with help from the various travel websites – lists of useful website given at the end. You can also find out from traveler accounts of people who have already travelled to that part of India – just Google.

7. Choice Of Stay

You will find a number of high-end hotels with international amenities in the four metropolis and other big cities in India. In other parts you will find cheaper stay options, which will also provide with basic necessities. Of late there has been a rise in the number of resorts in all the major tourist attractions. Many places also offer guest houses and even home-stay facilities now-a-days. Apart from these, there are also the YWCA and YMCA has hostels in different locations across India.

8. Book Your Hotel or Hostel

A good idea is to always book in advance the hotels or any of the other places you want to stay in. The travel websites often have good deals for hotels as well which you can make use of. A list of travel websites are given at the end.

9. Finding Toilet Paper

There are no guarantees that you will find toilet papers in the toilets around the country. The bigger hotels, airports and lounges might have them but other places you can never be sure. So if you have to use toilet paper then carry some with you always. Also, remember not to dispense the paper in the commode, instead use the bin next to the toilet for that as these toilets get clogged by papers.
The Indian alternative of using water to clean up is good but then again at most places you won't find soap to clean your hands afterwards. If you are happy using the water then carry some soap with you.

10. Using The Squat Toilet

Though the situation is changing, squat toilets are the most common ones found in India. The western commode is slowly making its way in, however use your discretion to use one. If you are uncomfortable using the squat toilet then enquire about the type of toilet before booking your accommodation.

"In religion, India is the only millionaire - the One land that all men desire to see, and having seen once, by even a glimpse, would not give that glimpse for all the shows of all the rest of the globe combined"
- Mark Twain

11. Get A Pick-up

The hotels usually arrange for a pick-up from railway stations or airports on request. If you are travelling alone or with children, if you are reaching your destination at odd hours, this facility comes in very useful. Be aware of your travel time and make use of hotel pick-ups, just inform them at least a day in advance.

12. Payments At Hotels

If you are staying at a premium hotel you can use your credit card to make the payments. If you are staying in budget hotels or home-stays you might have to pay in cash. Enquire beforehand about the preferred mode of transaction and be prepared.

13. Accommodating Children

In budget hotels across India children below 12 years are expected to share the parents' bed and usually for free. However you could ask for extra beds for a nominal fee. The premium hotels would arrange children's accommodation more readily.

14. Babysitter

To enjoy a night out with your partner you can engage the services of a paid babysitter arranged by the premium hotel. Even in budget hotels they find reliable persons to look after your kid while you are out. These services are all available on request and the hotel should be informed beforehand.

15. Local Sightseeing

On request the hotel will arrange for cars and drivers for local sightseeing trips. These drivers are from that are so they can double duty as tour guides as well. You can ask for an English speaking driver and with luck you will get someone who can manage a few words.

16. Book Travel Tickets

Book your travel tickets in advance. In India you can buy reserved train tickets as much as four months in advance. However, there is a provision of reserving tickets in the nick of time at a higher price called 'tatkal', but this is difficult to get without travel agents. Air tickets too are pretty much booked well in advance. To eliminate ticket reservation issues try to reserve your place in the trains or planes before you reach the country.

India – Food Guide

17. Win Over The Spices

Indian food is spicy. You could ask about the spiciness of dishes before ordering them. In the Southern parts of the country you will find a dish "Curd rice" which is a mix of boiled rice and curd which will help to cut down the heat. In Northern India you can order rice and curd separately for the same purpose. Besides this, you should try the local food in places you visit to find out the flavors of India. You can also enjoy the various fresh fruits on offer while on the road. The sweet *chai* with a few glucose biscuits should keep you filled for short time as well.

18. International Food Chains

If you are full of Indian food and want to eat something that you are familiar with don't worry. Pizzas, burgers and noodles are available in almost all places now, US restaurant chains like McDonalds, Pizza Hut, Subway and KFC have branches in most of the places. Albeit, these places offer Indian versions of these food types too.

19. Drinking Water

At all given times stick to drinking sterilized water. However, ensure the bottle has proper sealed cap and/or the plastic wrapper around the cap. There are instances of bottle tempering where the bottles are filled with tap water and capped back on.
Another trick is to carry a SteriPEN – the portable water purifier, so you could purify your water on your own. Else you can use the various water purifier tablets like Aquatabs to get safe drinking water.

20. Eat Cooked Food

Make a point to eat only cooked food in India. Cooking kills most of the germs and gives you a safer dish. Eat from a busy hotel with good turnover – ask the locals for the best hotel in town. Avoid the salads, juices and ice in whatever you eat or drink. For fruits, stick to the peel and eat varieties or carry your own small knife to cut and eat instead of buying cut fruits from the vendors.

21. Go Veg

In India you will find the majority of the population to be vegetarian. Though in certain parts fish is what the locals will swear by. Stick to vegetarian food that will help to keep the tummy in shape. If you do want to give the non-veg dishes a shot go to the most popular eatery or the high end places.

22. Use Hands For Eating

This is how they eat in India and you must follow eating with hands too, it is fun. Besides being fun, washing hands to clean them up is easy. You can never be sure of the utensils though. A good practice is to wipe your dish with a paper towel before serving food on that.

23. Avoid Overeating

As tasty as the food might be, avoid overeating. That is the number one cause for upset stomach. Having an upset stomach on a travel is the worst thing you can have. Carry supplements which help digestion and use in case you feel you have over eaten.

24. Avoid Street Food

As tempting as some street food joints might look, avoid them. Though the locals enjoy and not get affected by germs in those places things might be different for you. Their immunity is build to resist those. However, if you have to try the street food, choose a busy vendor. Also look for vendors which are favored by the local families – if that is safe for their family that should be safe for you too.

25. Enjoy A *Thali*

A *thali* or plate is one big plate with an array of local delicacies put together – a complete local meal. These *thali's* are usually cost effective and offer the local flavor at one go. These are often unlimited, that is they keep refilling without any extra cost, thereby increasing chances of overeating. You should try at least one *thali* during your trip to India.

26. Enjoy A Home Dinner

While on a trip you will get a chance to make local friends and they will surely invite you home for lunch or dinner. For the ladies of India one good way to show their love or appreciation is to fill you up with food. The trick is to eat slowly while making conversation. Food usually will be super tasty but if you eat fast they will keep refilling and probably force feed you. So keep a tab on the quantity and enjoy!

India – Customs, Etiquette And Propriety

27. Dress Appropriately

People in most parts of India are conservative; dressing modestly is therefore advised to all, especially women. You can wear long cotton pants which run below the knees and tops which preferably cover your bottom. You can buy the Indian top and pants dress called as 'suit' or 'salwar kameez', get the light cotton material which are good for the weather as well. Also, remember to carry a long scarf at all times, that could come in handy for covering up where ever needed.

28. Follow Instructions At Tourist Places

Most of the tourist attractions like the Taj Mahal, have a separate queue for the foreigners to buy tickets. The ticket prices vary too. Some of these places charge different fee for still photography and videos, note these and pay accordingly. Another point to note, refrain taking pictures in temples as in most of these places photography is forbidden.

29. Remove Shoes At Entrance To Temples

You will not be allowed to enter the temple premises with shoes or sandals, if you leave them unattended at the entrance good chances are you won't see them again. Most of the temples have a shoe office near the entrance where you can deposit your shoes for safekeeping for a meager amount. You could also keep your shoes under the safeguard of the various little shops around the temples. You could however, keep your socks on to keep your feet safe from sun exposed hot rock floors of some of these places.

30. Cover Your Head At Religious Places

Most of the religious places in India require you to cover your head, specially the females. Even the males need to cover their head in certain temples, gurudwaras, mazaars and mosques. Ladies keep handy a scarf or the Indian *dupatta* – a scarf like piece of cloth used on top of a suit, while men could use their kerchief for the same use.

31. Forget About Personal Space

With such a huge population the concept of personal space is non-existent. Do not feel threatened by the host of people surrounding you. Being a foreigner you will attract some curious onlookers some might even walk up to you for a chat. If you want to cut off from the surroundings, the noise and people use an iPod while moving around. Create that personal space in your head.

32. Understand The Interesting Head Wobbles

The head wobbles are an interesting way of communication across the country. Overall when the head nod is towards the front that means agreement and nod to the sides mean no. However, there are hundreds of other wobbles whose meaning ranges from acceptance to appreciation to showing gratitude, this you can only observe and absorb. Once you understand you would find the wobble easy and even natural.

33. Learn The Local Language

There are 22 officially recognized languages in India with their hundred different variations. Hindi is the most widely understood language. Before travelling to India learn few basic words and phrases in Hindi like Hello = *Na-mas-te*, thank you = *shuk-riya*, water = *pani*, let's go = *cha-liye*, stop = *ruko*.
If your travel plans are restricted to one area of India, you could even pick out the major language there and learn a few words. The locals appreciate when a foreigner tries to speak their tongue and are more than willing to help you out.

34. Interacting With The Opposite Sex

Do not touch people of the opposite sex to greet or to show affection. Women are advised to not interact in an overly friendly manner with local men, as that is taken as a pick-me-up signal. Be guided by your instincts and be cautious of people you are interacting with.

35. Be Careful With Your Hands And Feet

Try not to touch people of things with your feet. If you do so then apologize promptly because in India feet are considered to be dirty so when you touch something with your feet or point your feet towards someone that is impolite behavior.
Similarly, using left hand to pass on things or using left hand for eating is considered disrespectful and odd respectively.

36. Understand That Time Is Relative

Blame it on the traffic or the take it easy mentality of the people be sure to wait for things to happen. If someone asks you to wait for five minutes that could mean waiting for as much as half hour even. Things do take their own sweet time to happen; you need to have patience to wait.

37. Feel Like A Celebrity

You will get numerous requests for photographs to be clicked with the locals, especially if you are travelling with children. You can feel like a celebrity and oblige the requests or just turn down the requests just like them. Whatever you do, do not show your frustration or anger on the streets; instead turn down the requests politely.

38. How Much To Tip

Tipping is not mandatory but you can tip the porter or bell boy in the hotels. Tip moderately, □.10 per bag should be decent enough. Apart from this if you feel any service by anyone praiseworthy then you could tip whatever you wish to. At restaurants you can tip 10-20% of the bill or not pay anything if you did not like the food.

39. Be Part Of The Festivals

In India there is no dearth of festivals, every month there is some festival at some part of the country. Most of these festivals are celebrated as community events where people come together to celebrate as a large group. As a result all of these events are very noisy, chaotic, colorful and fun at the same time. Festivals also come with their own nuances and food items. If you happen to be present during any of the festival do take part and enjoy the event.
Some of the important festivals in the Indian calendar are Lohri (Jan), Holi (March), Ratha yatra (July), Onam (Aug), Ganesh Chaturthi (Sept), Diwali (Oct/Nov), Durga puja/Dussera (Oct/Nov), Christmas (Dec).

India – Safety Norms

40. Display Your Wedding Band

The ever inquisitive Indian will question you about your marital status; the best answer to give is "married", always. Indians promptly judge people who are not married, women especially. This also announces that you are unavailable, acting as a safeguard against unwanted attention from men. Even if you are not married sporting a band on your finger and maintaining you are married is a good strategy.

41. Avoid Going Out At Night

Night outs for women travelling alone should be ruled out. You will find very few women on the road after sun down. However, if you are in a group or with local friends you could step out with confidence.

42. Raise Your Voice

If someone annoys you and would not leave you alone raising your voice will do the trick. Most of these people will step back when the target makes noise and attracts attention of people around. They are afraid of losing face in front of the local people. Moreover, there will be at least one helpful person to bail you out of the situation.

43. Be Prepared To Fight Back

On a solo trip keep handy a safety pouch with pepper spray, a Swiss knife and a whistle. This is applicable for all places including India. Keeping your defenses ready and being prepared to fight adversary is necessary for your own safety.

44. Refrain From Carrying Too Much Cash

Pick-pocketing is a living art in the crowded streets of India. Foreigners are also considered loaded targets – whether you have money or not. Therefore, avoid carrying huge amount of cash or other valuable items with you always.

45. Keep A Calm Head

Bargaining in the market is fun but at times that might get ugly. There are some markets where if you open your mouth once you will have to purchase something from the shop. When in a market keep your eyes and ears open and be aware of your surroundings. Keep away from haggling too much. Most importantly, keep your head calm, be firm but polite, that should keep you out of trouble.

46. Keep Your Mobile Handy

Mobile phone these days are pretty useful and life saving as well. Keep your phone with you at all times. If you are travelling alone make a call to your friends giving details of the vehicle you are travelling in – auto rickshaw or taxi cab within the driver's earshot. Even if someone is not responding on the other side enact such a conversation. This will alert the driver and you will not get into any trouble with him.

India – Shoppers Stop

47. Explore Before Buying

Each market has a large number of shops selling similar things. Explore the market and compare prices before making your purchases. You can even talk to the locals or people in the hotel about the rates to find out if you are being ripped.

48. Ship Purchases Home

If you are purchasing heavy items or things in bulk some shops arrange the goods to be delivered at your home. Find out from fellow travelers or your local contacts if the shop is reliable. Ensure you get a proper receipt and contact details before committing to such systems.

49. Enjoy Bargaining Like Indians

Observe how the locals are bargaining, try yourself too and have fun. The trick is to start really low and then jump a little high at a time. Keep the conversation light and fun to avoid unpleasant situations. If you do not want to get into all this hassle then buy things from fixed priced shops which are usually fair priced.

50. Know What To Buy

There are unlimited number of items flooding the Indian market that would lure you to buy them. Best things to buy here are textiles – across the country there are various dresses, shawls, bedspread of high quality cotton, silk and wool. Then you will find a very wide range of arts and crafts goods, again the specializations differ from region to region and each one has its own aesthetic appeal. One other thing to buy from India is jewelry - the designs are beautiful with delicate work in stones and pearls.

Other Helpful Resources

http://www.asherfergusson.com/2012/11/100-tips-to-survive-travel-through-india-fun-facts-culture-temples-pictures-more/
http://www.indiamike.com/
http://www.roughguides.com/destinations/asia/india/
http://www.indiacelebrating.com/festivals/

For Tickets And Hotels

https://www.irctc.co.in/eticketing/loginHome.jsf
http://www.makemytrip.com/
http://www.yatra.com/

How Many 50 Things to Know Books Have You Read?

Created by Lisa Rusczyk. Click here to visit 50 Things to Know on Amazon to see the many 50 Things to Know Books. Please visit us on Facebook, twitter, and Pinterest.

50 Things to Know to Get Things Done Fast: Easy Tips for Success

50 Things to Know to Organize Your Life: A Quick Start Guide to Declutter, Organize, and Live Simply

50 Things to Know About Being a Minimalist: Downsize, Organize, and Live Your Life

50 Things to Know About Speed Cleaning: How to Tidy Your Home in Minutes

Contact Information

50 THINGS TO KNOW

Website: 50 Things to Know
Facebook: Follow 50 Things to Know on Facebook
Pinterest: 50 Things to Know on Pinterest
YouTube: Watch 50 Things to Know on YouTube
Twitter: Follow 50 Things to Know on Twitter
Mailing List: Join the 50 Things to Know Mailing List to Learn About New Releases

About The Author

Manidipa Bhattacharyya is a creative writer and editor, with an education in English literature and Linguistics. After working in the IT industry for seven long years she decided to call it quits and follow her heart instead. Manidipa has been ghost writing, editing, proof reading and doing secondary research services for many story tellers and article writers for about three years. She stays in Kolkata, India with her husband and a busy two year old. On her own time Manidipa enjoys travelling, photography and writing flash fiction.

Hailing from India, it was a pleasure to put together these points for someone who will be coming to this land for the first time. As I explored the various travelogues I found things people have mentioned which normally as residents in the country do not pop-up to us. Writing this book has made me proud of my country all over again and also pulled up points which we should improve upon as a country.

Made in the USA
San Bernardino, CA
03 December 2018